Hide-and-Seek

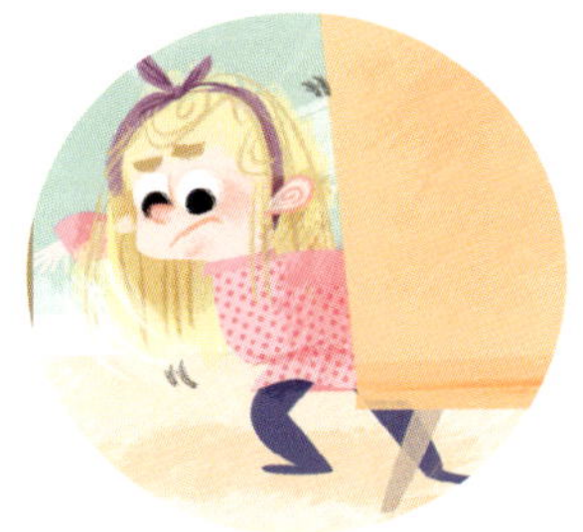

Written by
Stephen Rickard

Illustrated by
Mez Clark

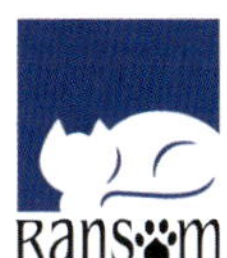

Ransom

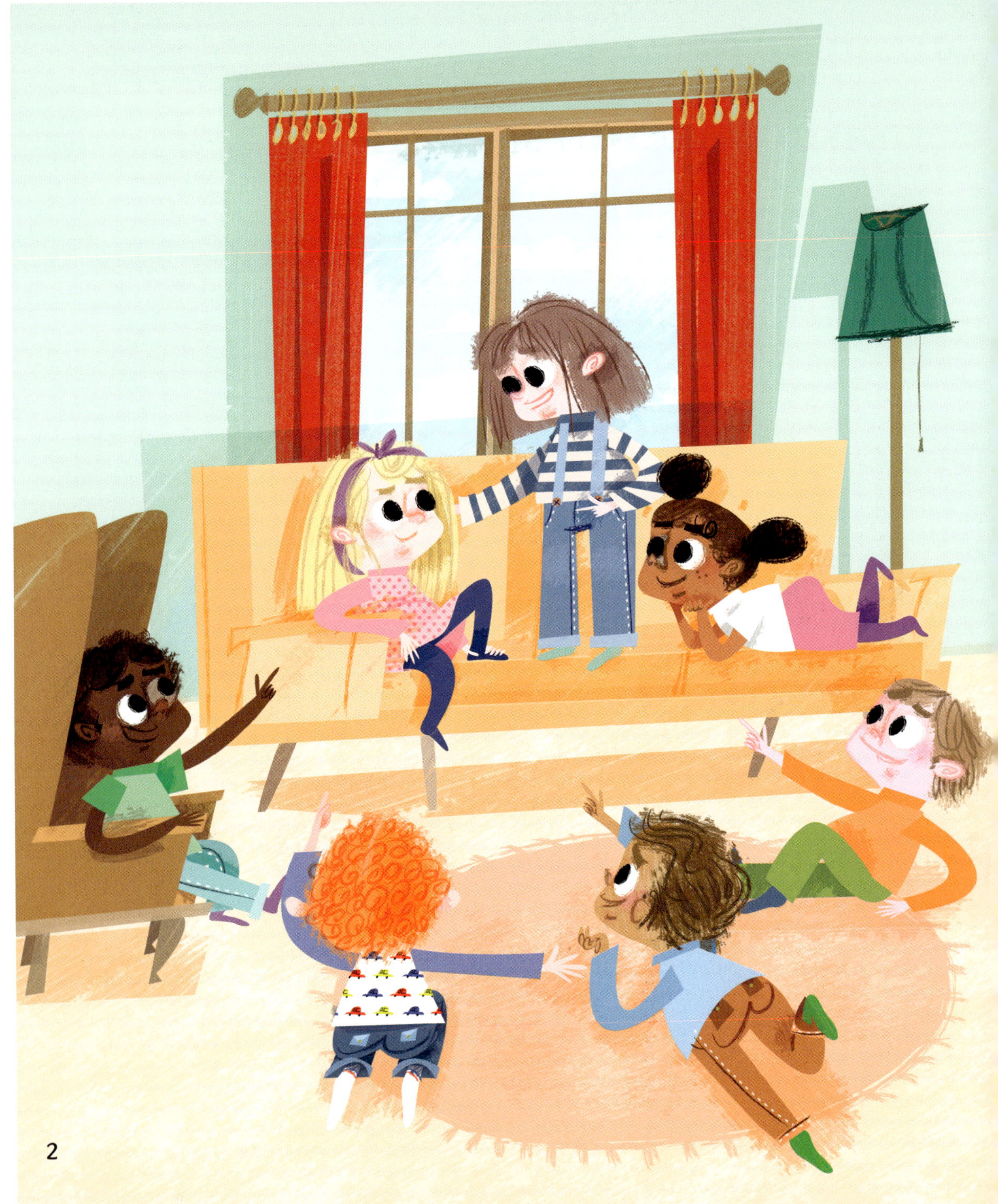

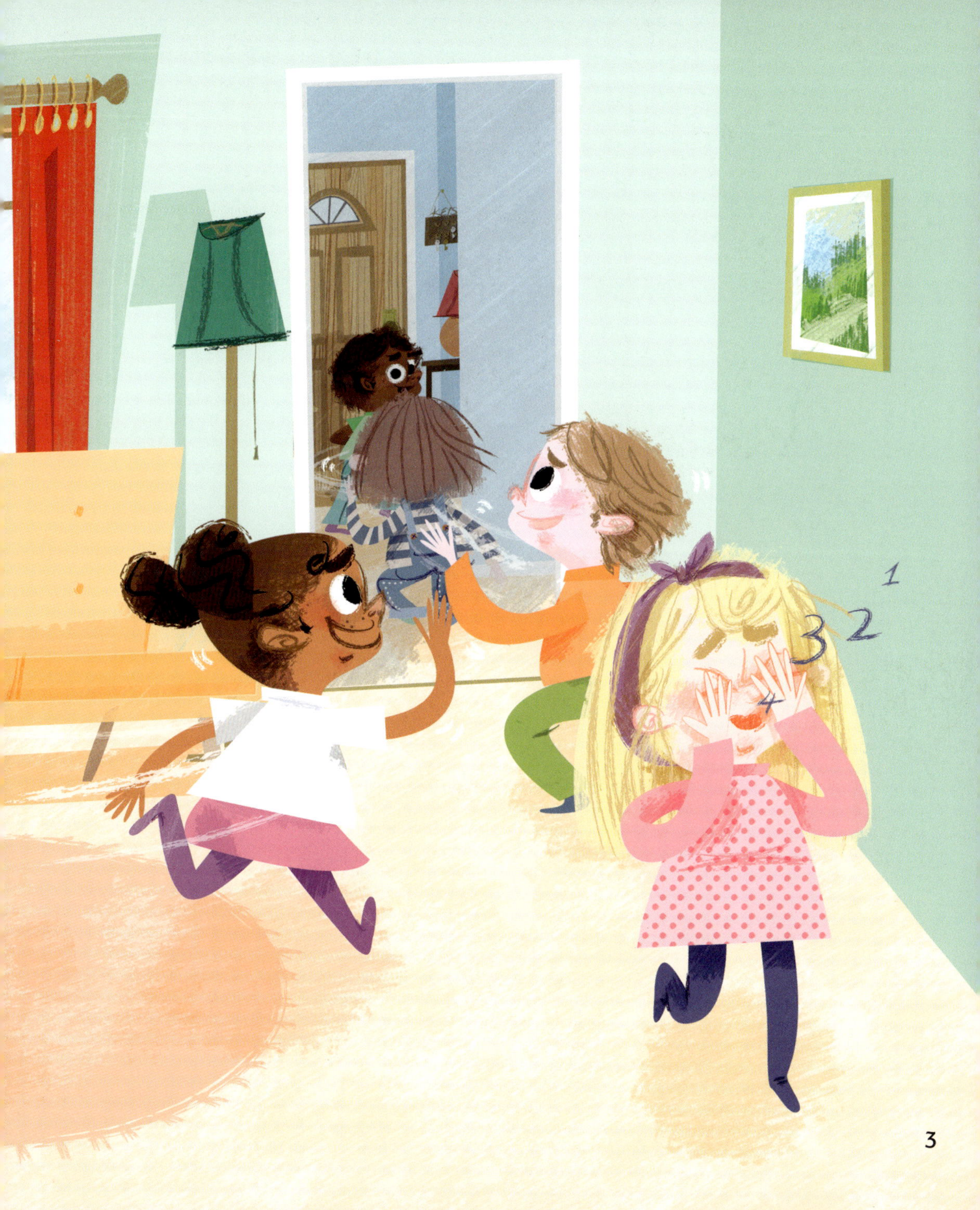
1
2
3
4

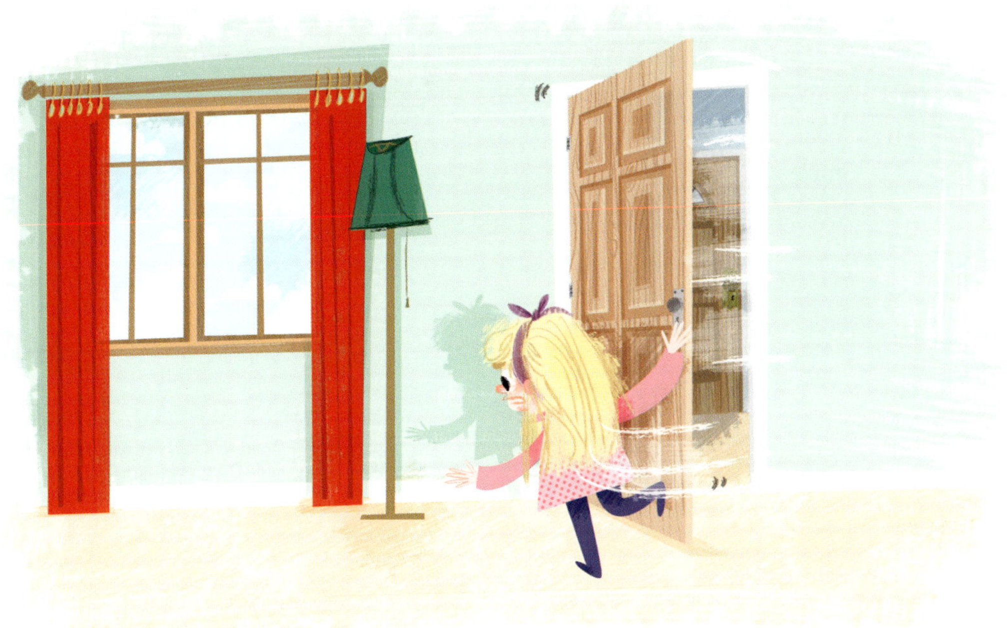

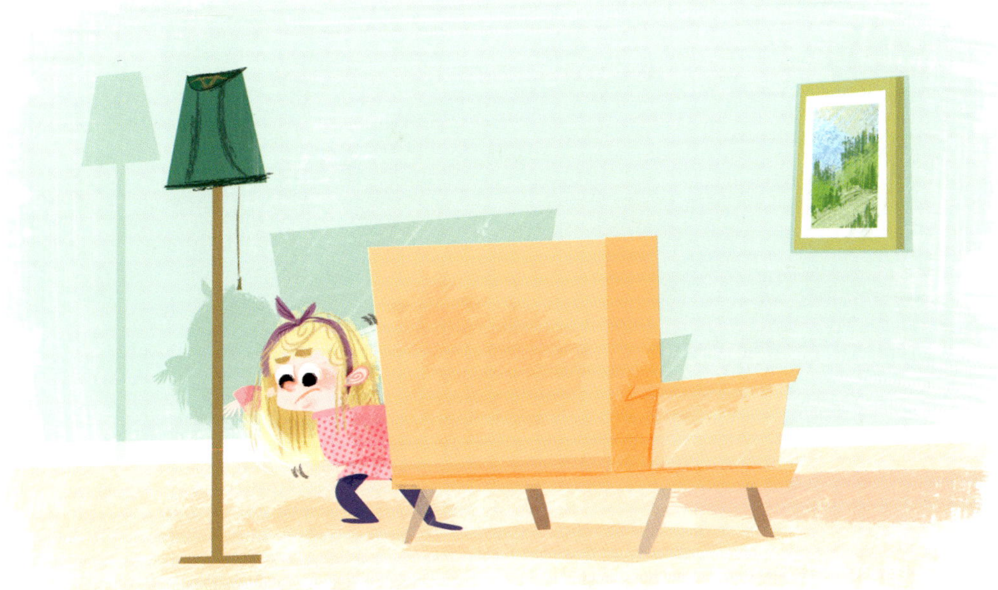

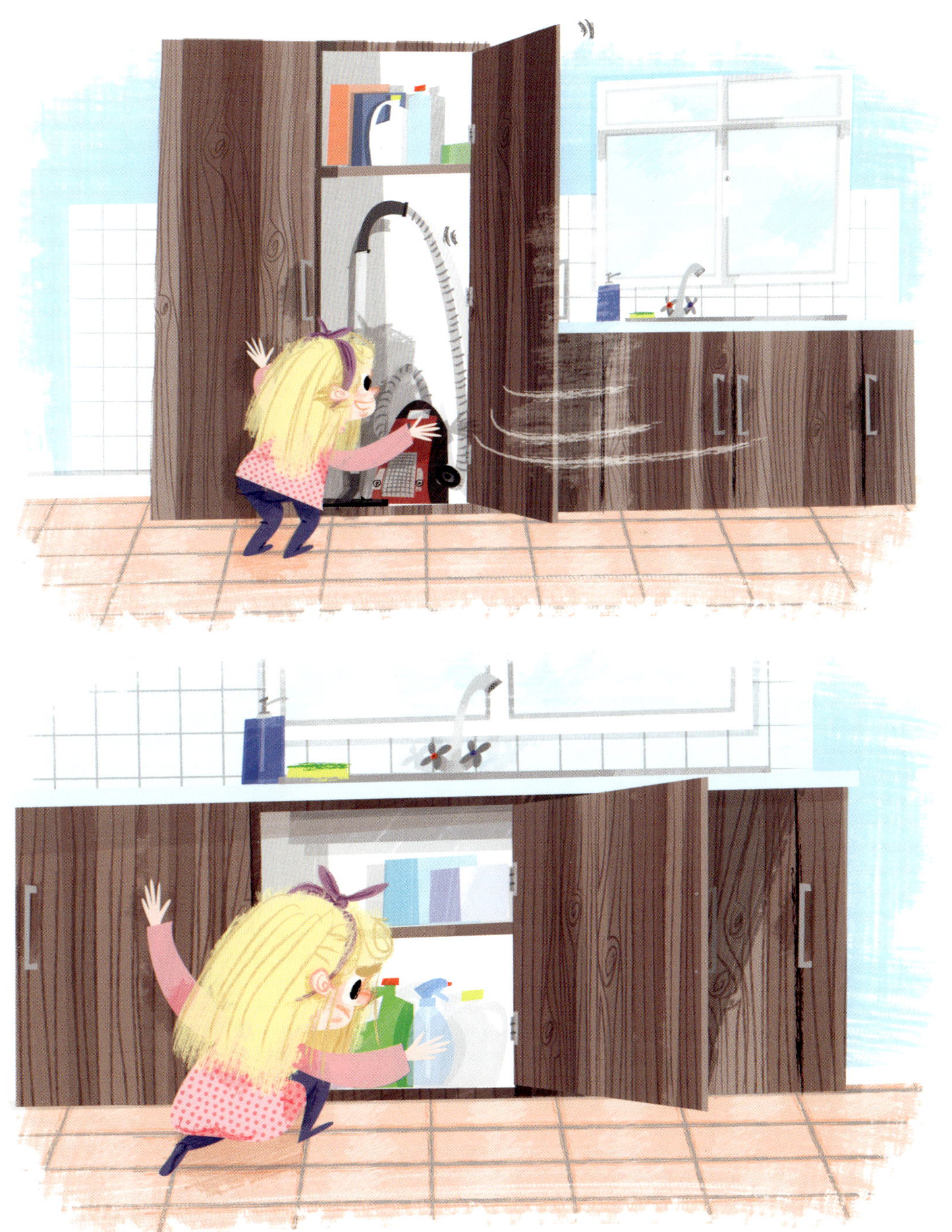

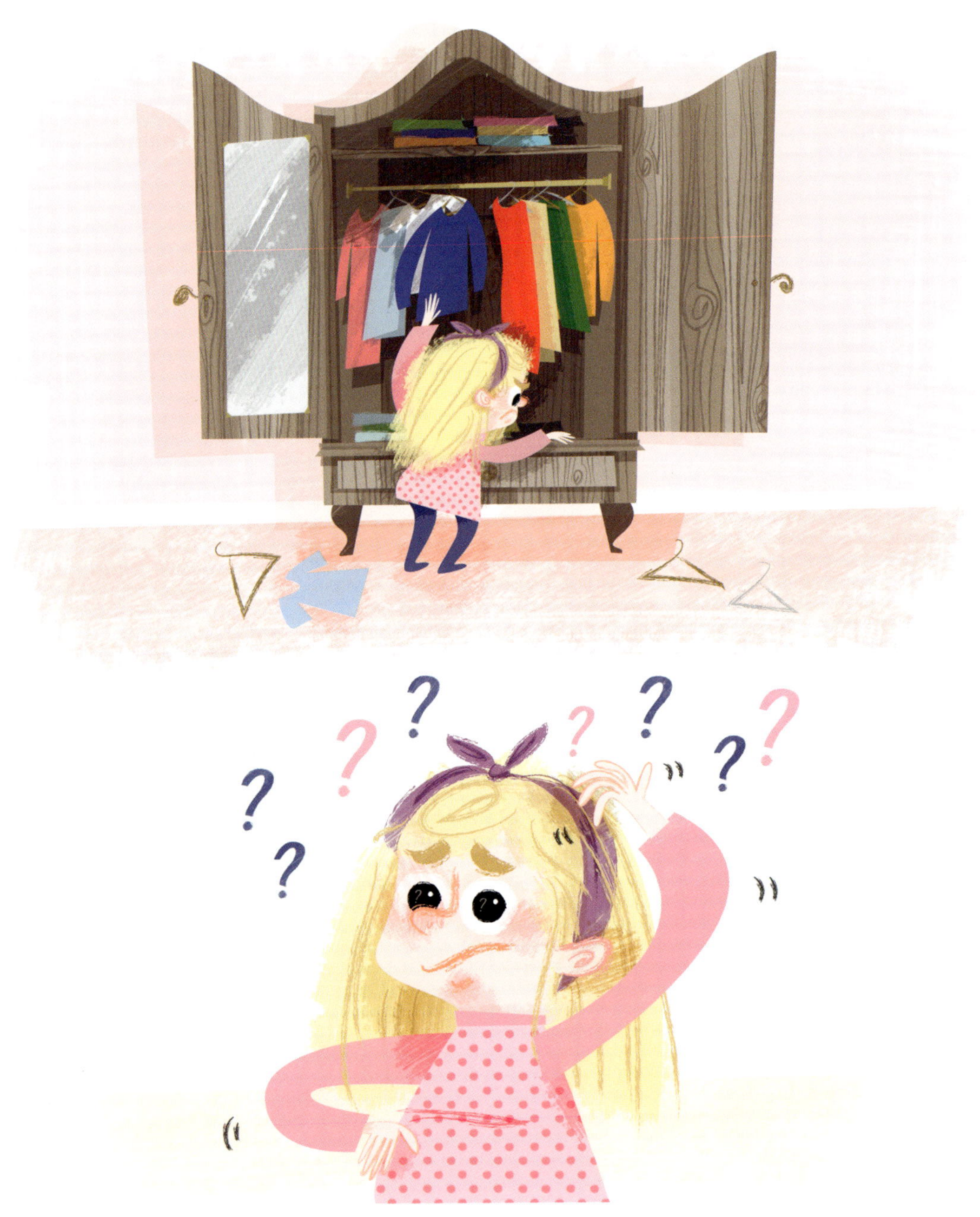

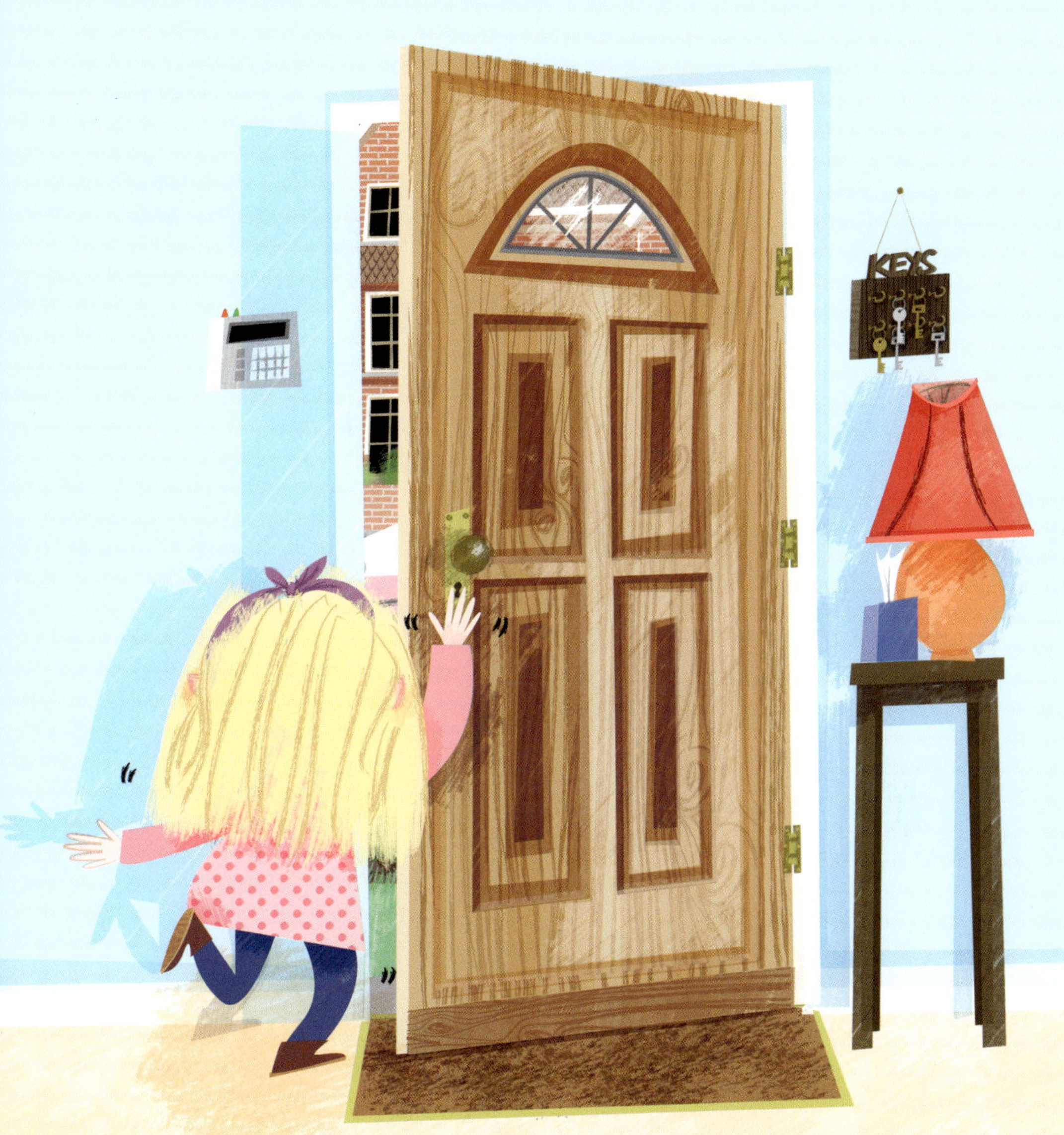
KEYS

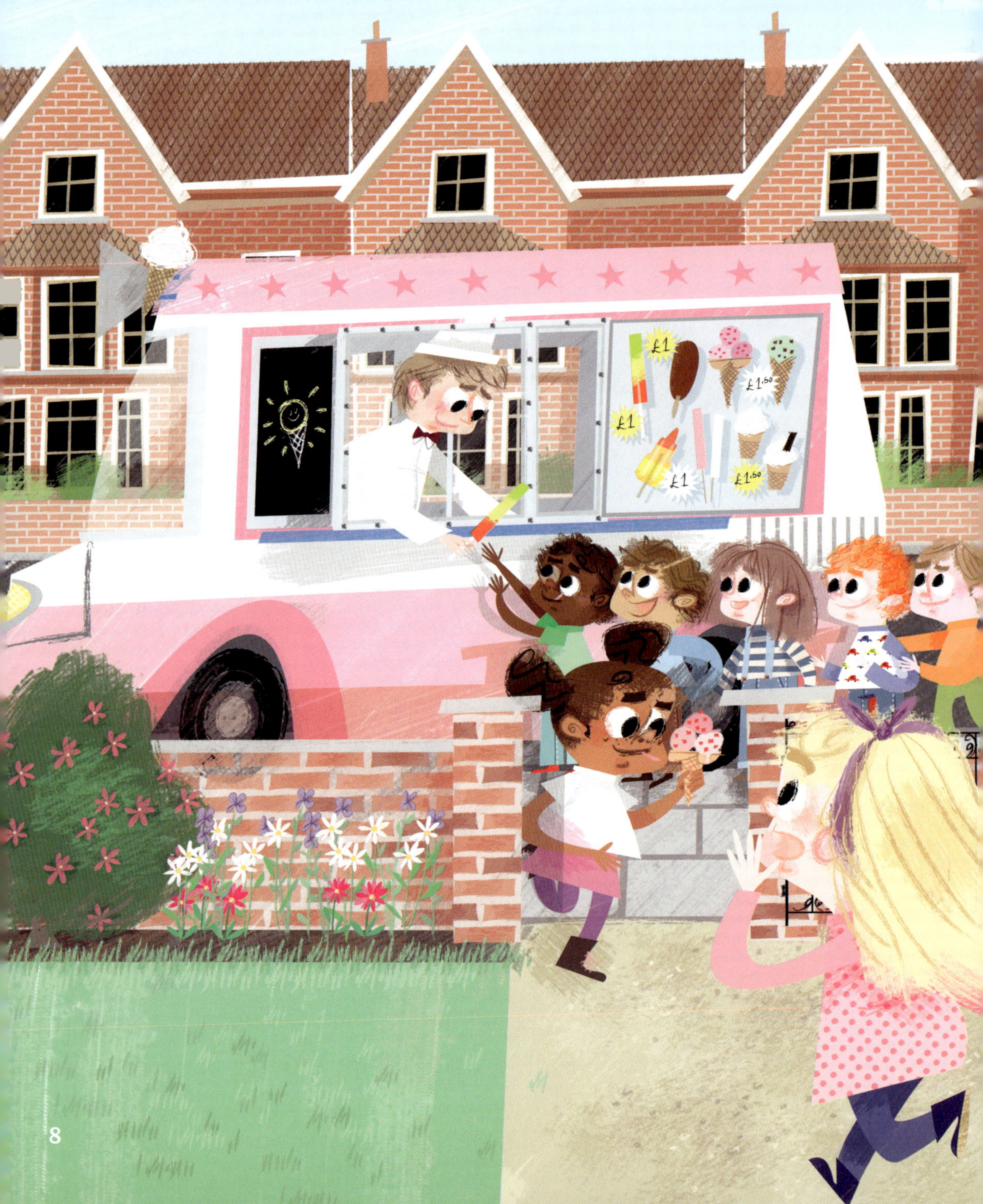

£1
£1
£1.50
£1
£1.50
£1